1

CHAPTER

INTRODUCTION

African Giant Land Snails are one of the most fascinating creatures in the world. A typical African giant snail consists of the upper body (head), lower body (foot), and outer body (shell). The shell plays a huge role in the life of the snail. It holds its visceral mass. The visceral mass is the softest part of the Snail which includes the heart, stomach, lungs, kidney, and other vital organs. These vital organs are covered by a tissue inside the snail called a mantle.

The Upper Body (Head)

The snail's upper body (head) bears sensory organs like its pair of retractable tentacles. One is long and the other one is typically shorter. The longer tentacle holds the eyes which the snail uses to distinguish light and darkness, while the shorter tentacle is the organ of smell and touch. The mouth is in the center of the snail's head, just under the short tentacle.

The Lower Body (Foot)

The lower body consists of a muscular disc-like foot. This is located under the head of the snail. Snails use this part of their body to move. They do so by extending it so that it clings to objects, allowing the snail to drag the rest of its body after it.

Chu Obike is the President and founder of Extensive Agricultural Research and Consulting Initiative, a division of CH Agro Allied Industry. He is an Author and an agricultural scientist and consultant who has expert hands-on knowledge and has done extensive research on Animal Husbandry.

He has written many articles and presented papers at many seminars and workshops on fields like Snail Farming, Poultry Farming, Bee farming, Pig farming, and other livestock farming. He is also the Author of numerous fiction books like the bestseller Victims of Circumstance.

For information on booking Chu Obike please visit ChuObike.com
Also by Chu Obike
Victims of Circumstance
The Five Leprous Fingers

CONTENTS

Besides using their lower body to move, they also use their lower body (foot) for crawling, swimming, and burrowing into the ground to lay eggs or to hide from predators. In addition, snails also use their foot for engulfing food substances into their mouth.

The Outer Body (Shell)

The shell is a calcareous covering made of calcium. This calcium is produced within the organs and secreted through the mantle. The shell is the snail's first line of defense against attack from predators. When a snail is attacked by a predator or when it senses danger, it can withdraw into its shell, the shell encloses the snail completely.

The shell also provides the right environment for the snail to thrive and survive by providing the first line of defense against enemies. The snail's shell enlarges as it advances in age and size. The shell protects the snail from physical damage, predators, and from dehydration. Snails need to stay hydrated to be healthy and function effectively.

2
CHAPTER
SNAIL HOUSING

The best way to raise African Giant Land Snails is in snail houses. Snail houses can be big or small. Snail houses are easy to construct. They can be built with wood or cement blocks. The size, shape, and positioning of doors and windows vary based on the topography of the land and the available space. Snail houses should be designed as much as possible to replicate a snail's natural habitat. An ideal snail house is built in a way that the snails and their food sources (plants & vegetables) co-exist.

For snail houses, it is important that the roofing be done with iron netting. The netting holes should be small enough to not only keep predators out but also prevent the snails from crawling out—especially young African Giant Land Snails. Roof netting is an essential part of duplicating a natural habitat for several reasons.

First, netting is essential for adequate ventilation and natural temperature control. This eliminates the need for an enclosed roof. With the top of the snail house now open except for the netting, the temperature in the snail house will naturally be regulated. This will ensure a thriving ecosystem for not only the African Giant Land Snails but also for their food source (the plants and vegetables) that co-exist with them.

The sun shines directly into the snail house, facilitating photosynthesis. Also, during rainy periods, rainfall can enter directly into the housing, reducing the amount of labor associated with manually watering the plants. It will also help to reduce the amount of time it will take new snails to readjust to a farm environment when they are brought in from an outside source. In addition, it will make the snails feel as if they are in their natural habitat.

Secondly, netting restrains young Snails within the snail house. The iron netting will prevent the African Giant Land Snails, especially the young snails, from crawling out. Note however, that snails within a snail house can sometimes huddle together, so great care should be taken when building the iron netting roof to make sure that the netting is tight, compact, and securely fitted so that the weight of the snails as they are huddle together does not compromise or break the netting. In other words, the netting should be adequately fitted so that there will be no holes or spaces wide or weak enough to break or tear for the snails to crawl out or for their predators to crawl in.

After securing the flooring of the snail housing, ordinary sandy soil should be introduced into the housing to a height of at least 5 cm to 6 cm (approximately 2 inches x 2.5 inches). It is this soil that will be used by the snails to lay their eggs

Another key factor when considering a snail house is the flooring structure. Snail houses can have wooden floors or concrete (cement) floors. Snails can burrow (making a tunnel) therefore, snail houses with wood floors should be firmly boarded to avoid this. Concrete (cement) floors are best for preventing snails from burrowing out of their housing.

Snails usually lay inside the ground (soil) at a depth of about 2 to 4 cm (approximately 1 inch x 2 inches) deep. Snail eggs mature and hatch on their own without parental care. When the eggs hatch, the little snails crawl out of the soil on their own without help from the parent snail. Adequate flooring layered with enough sandy soil and natural temperature will ensure that this independent process is completed successfully.

The soil introduced into the snail house has another advantage in that the snail farmer can also use it to grow certain plants and vegetables inside the farm enclosure that the snails can consume. It is important for snail farmers to water the plants and vegetables inside the snail house, especially during the non-rainy seasons. Small-scale farmers can also rear snails in drums, tanks, and wooden cages. In these cases, care must be taken to customize and prepare the chosen habitat to suit the African Giant Land Snails.

Farmers choosing to use drums, tanks or wooden cages should be careful not to overcrowd the snails. Adequate space should be provided for the snails to lay eggs and move around.

Key factors, such as creating the right environment with adequate ventilation, space, drainage, and other things should be considered when using smaller housing structures.

3

CHAPTER

SELECTING YOUR SNAIL STOCK

A good snail farm starts with a good selection of healthy snails. Care must be taken when selecting a parent stock or starting stock. The best-starting stock of African Giant Land Snails should be obtained from existing farms or hunted in the wild or their natural habitat.

Selecting a healthy stock of snails as a starting stock will avoid problems like introducing diseases into the farm. It will also allow for quick and easy adaptation of the snails to the new farm. In addition to selecting a healthy parent stock, care must also be taken to maintain a decent level of hygiene in the snail farm by implementing active sanitation measures such as disinfecting before encountering the snails and consistently fumigating the farm to control diseases and avoid infestation of insects such as ants. It is also essential to avoid unnecessary entry of non-farm workers into the snail house.

Snail farms that are exposed to diseases take time and resources to manage and control as they lead to a mass dying of the snails. Farmers dealing with disease infestation within the farm will need to carefully examine the snail stock daily and separate the disease-infected ones from the healthy ones until the situation is under control.

It is more efficient to take preventive measures when selecting your starting stock by avoiding carelessly sourcing your parent stock from anywhere, than to deal with a disease outbreak in the farm. While choosing your starting stock, it is also important to avoid buying snails hung along the roadside (as seen in many third world countries), or those sold inside a market since they cannot give you value having been starved of food and water and very often exposed to bad climatic conditions. Snails that are starved of food and nutrition often retreat into hibernation.

It takes time, effort, and resources to acclimate any snails in this condition into a snail farm environment. Snails that are sourced from existing snail farms will very often adjust rapidly to a new farm environment with no downtime, and immediately adapt, function, and begin to contribute to the new farm ecosystem. In other words, they will require little or no effort to manage, as they most often adjust to the new environment quickly.

It is also important to note that the temperature inside the snail farm is regularly monitored and adjusted to make the Snails comfortable (especially during hot/dry periods).

The open-roof snail housing is very advantageous in this regard as it naturally allows rainfall and sunshine to come in. However, during the season when the atmosphere tends to be dry, it is important to water the snail farm by installing sprinkler systems, to ensure that the snails and their food sources continue to flourish.

Another key factor is to avoid sourcing snails with damaged shells. Snails with damaged shells or any serious body damage bring low productivity when introduced into a farm as it takes time and effort for them to heal.

4

CHAPTER

TYPES OF FOOD

African Giant Land Snails by nature are omnivorous; they feed on little crawling animals like earthworms, and diverse types of vegetables, grains, and fruits. They especially like soft, watery, and powdery fruits. Bigger snails, when not well-fed, cannibalize younger snails by engulfing the little ones into their mouth and feeding on them. But this is in extreme cases when the snails are not well-fed and are hungry.

In ideal conditions inside the farm, well-fed snails prefer vegetables, fruits, and grains. They include water leaves, pawpaw leaves, pawpaw fruits, pap made from maize, or the chaff of the maize remaining after extracting pap from it.

Snails also like cassava leaves, and cocoyam leaves. Snail farmers are advised (as they become confident handling snails within their farm) to experiment with other types of vegetables, fruits, and grains to see if the snails will eat them. Farmers should do this with great vigilance while carefully observing the types of foods the snails respond positively to.

If snails are to grow and produce eggs very well, then the best types of foods available should be given to them. Research has shown that vegetables and grains are good for African Giant Land Snails. Snails that feed on them produce better healthy eggs.

Snail farmers bringing snails from other farms to either grow their stock or as starter stock should find out the types of foods they have been previously given so that the same can be continued. Farmers can also, if necessary, gradually change their diet to the regular diet in their farm.

Clean water in a container must always be made available inside the farm as Snails require a regular supply of clean and cool water.

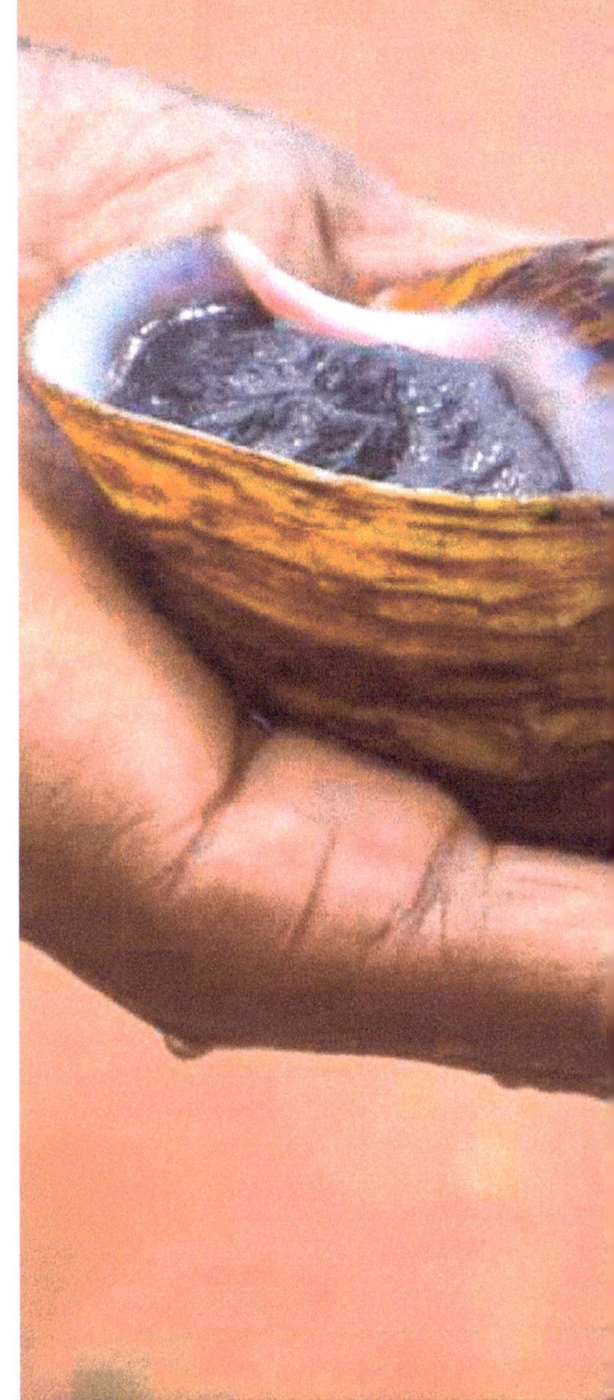

5

CHAPTER

GROWTH & REPRODUCTION

The full reproductive maturity circle of African Giant Land Snails can be reached between four to eight months depending on how well the snails are fed. If snails are well fed, their visceral mass which contains all their reproductive and digestive organs also enlarges and they increase in weight.

A snail can start producing eggs no matter its age if the weight reaches 90 grams—135 grams. Their best breeding periods are during the rainy seasons.
If snails are on a well-managed farm and are well-fed, they can produce all year round. Snails can live up to six years or even above that. Experts can easily determine the snail's age by studying the marked linings on its shell.

Snails are hermaphrodites, which means that they have both male and female reproductive organs in each of them. Although snails do mate, they can produce eggs with or without mating. They lay their eggs mostly at night, especially during rainy periods.

Also, when snails are well managed in the snail farm and the temperatures are regulated by the snail farmer to suit them, they can adjust and produce eggs all year round.

 Snails lay their eggs in clutches at about 2 cm deep. The depth at which their eggs are buried depends on the size of the eggs.

Their eggs are slippery to the touch and are oval almond-shaped with lemon-yellow shells. The typical hatch is between 25—45 days without parental care. At times, some of these eggs may take longer days to hatch.

Delay in hatching might be due to shell thickness, or high moisture content of the soil. In this case, artificial input can be made by the farmer through mechanical scarification of the egg at the top to make it easier for the young snail to emerge. Soil within the farm that has a high moisture content can be corrected by adding new sandy soil to the farm.

It is also important that the snail farmer reserve a small area for newly hatched snails. This will not only help the farmer monitor their growth and keep better records but also protect them from the bigger snails for safety.

Good nutrition is important if farmers want snails to produce at a fast rate.

Cannibalism can reduce the number of the farmers' stock and farmers should guard against bigger snails consuming smaller snails or engulfing their eggs by adequately feeding them.

Biological factors are important factors that snail farmers should guard against by adjusting the snails to the farm environment systematically so that they can produce all year (see chapter on biological makeup).

Old age can reduce the snail's reproductive capability and farmers should rectify this by selling off the old snails and replacing them with younger ones.

Weight loss is another factor that can affect a snail's reproductive capability and should be normalized through good foods rich in protein.

Effects of weather like rainfall and relative humidity affect the snails when they are in excess or not enough, so farmers should be observant of these temperature changes and adjust the farm accordingly.

6

CHAPTER

SNAIL FARM MANAGEMENT

Snail Farmers should regularly change the drinking water for the snails inside the snail house. Natural water sources such as boreholes, well water, stream water, or rainwater should be used for the African Giant Land Snails. Farmers must avoid chlorinated water, treated or purified water of any sort inside the farm.

Farmers should be vigilant in observing and inspecting their farms. Weak-looking or sick-looking snails inside the farm should immediately removed and isolated from the stock to avoid a disease outbreak from spreading out in the farm. People should not be allowed to enter snail farms unnecessarily.

Fresh sand and soil should be regularly introduced into the snail house to replenish the soil. But care should be taken not to disturb or break the laid eggs incubating inside the sand when fresh sand and soil are being introduced.

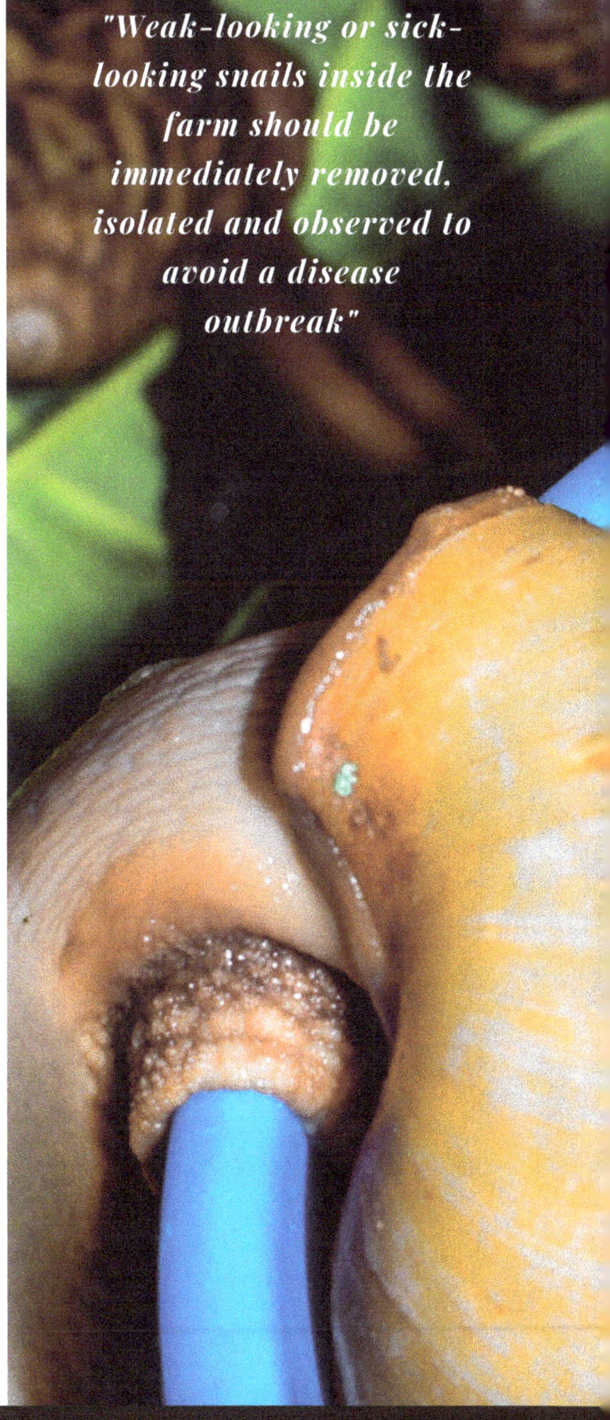

- Good record keeping is also vital. A good record book must be kept so that the farmer can monitor the progress of the farm and find out the areas that need improvement.

- Young snails should be removed from the snail house immediately after they emerge and taken to a reserved aread until they are big enough to be reintroduced back into the main farm.

- The farm must be kept clean and food debris removed from inside the snail house to avoid farm pollution by decayed food materials, which might cause an increase in soil acidity among other things.

- Using a sprinkle system or manually splashing the farm regularly with water during hot and dry seasons is essential.

- Snails are capable of burrowing out of the snail house. Farmers must watch against this by constructing good snail houses fortified with cemented floors.

- Farmers must avoid overstocking snails as this might lead to cannibalism, deaths, or even epidemics.

7

CHAPTER

MINIMIZING THREATS TO SNAILS

To ensure a healthy farm, farmers must understand some of the known hazards to African Giant Land Snails. One such hazard is treated or chlorinated water. This should be avoided around the snails.

Natural water sources are more adequate for African Giant Land Snails. Natural water sources include well water, stream water, rainwater, and other types of untreated water. Remember that water within a snail farm must be changed regularly to ensure a healthy habitat.

Raw Cement is also poisonous to African Giant Land Snails. Raw cement contains limestone. Limes stones are not favorable to African Giant Land Snails.

Comingling between other livestock on the farm can also be unhealthy for African Giant Land Snails. When other livestock are also contained within a farm, care should be taken to avoid cross-contamination. For example, poultry feeds mixed with lysine, methionine, and vitamins when mistakenly introduced into their drinking water also kill African Giant Land Snails.

So, care should be taken when handling poultry feed in the farm, most especially in farms where poultry stock or other livestock is also reared with African Giant Land Snails.

In the case of poultry feeds, it is recommended that farmers forget about poultry feeds altogether.

Animals and humans alike also pose a threat to African Giant Land Snails. African Giant Land Snails are proteinaceous, so animals naturally like to eat them. Snails tend to reproduce in large quantities, and they are edible by nature. Forest spiders, hawks, snakes, and moth larvae all feed on snails and their eggs. Humans also pose a risk to snails as snails are usually consumed as delicacies.

When snails meet hostility, they naturally withdraw into their shell. This is their first intuition, and it saves them from most of their enemies. In some cases, when they withdraw into the shells, the predator cannot access them. It is important to note that this instinct is not just for predators but also for survival when the environment is not conducive, such as in cases of rain.

Another way snails ward off attacks is by oozing out their slime. This slime can demobilize certain attackers. To minimize confronting hostile animals, snails are typically active at night.

Their nature of being active at night also gives them an edge over their natural enemies. They are shy animals by nature, so they are more confident operating at night. With time, however, snails in a farm environment learn to move around and eat all day round after they have observed the farm environment to be safe. Because of this, snails in the farm environment are naturally bigger than those in the wild, since they can eat all day and night and in all seasons.

Farmers must take adequate preventive measures to minimize these threats to African Giant Land Snails. Preventive measures such as regularly fumigating the farm, ensuring a decent level of sanitation, and minimizing unnecessary access to the farms should be established from the onset.

8

CHAPTER

BIOLOGICAL MAKE-UP

To run a successful snail farm, snail farmers must learn and understand them as much as possible. Snails operate within the seasons. Their body is functional mainly during the rainy and wet seasons. During dry seasons, or when their is not much water around they switch off (go into hibernation). Snails aestivate (become dormant) during these periods. They seal up their shells with calcium carbonate deposit and go to sleep.

Snail farmers can rearrange the snail's body mechanism during this period by making sure there is a constant water supply inside the snail house throughout the seasons. When snails are in the right atmosphere and where the environment is conducive, they will function and produce regardless of the season. In other words, they will not observe the change in the seasons.

Snails that are noticed that might be trying to switch off (going into hibernation), should be picked up every morning and immersed into the water where they will after some time peel off the calcium seal and crawl out and begin functioning.

The most efficient way to achieve this is by installing a sprinkler system or by manually splashing water inside the housing during hot seasons.

en there is enough moisture, coupled with a good
t high in minerals and protein, snails will eventually
pt inside their house and even reproduce during the
   seasons, as they cannot detect changes in their
ironment.

n important function of snails worth noting is their
lity to replace some of their damaged parts like
lacing worn-out teeth on the radial or if the shell
ch is secreted by the mantle is damaged, the mantle
nediately also repairs it. Lost eyes, tentacles, or even
 foot can all be replaced by the snail.

is important to note that the snail experts can
ermine age and arrested growth when they study the
rked lines on the shell and the shell also increases in
e as the visceral mass grows larger.

CHAPTER

9

LOCAL AND INTERNATIONAL MARKETS

...can Giant Land Snails are edible. They remain one of ... choice delicacies in most countries. The few snails ... are on sale in these countries are hunted in the ...ods and brought to the city markets to be sold. The ...il market opportunity has not been fully exploited by ...mers.

...e few hunted snails on sale are mainly sold during the ...ny season when the snails come out of aestivation and ...ve around. But most snail businesses stop during the ... seasons when no snails are moving about in the ...ods. These periods are the ideal time for snail farmers ... make good money since snails attract high prices ...ing the dry and hot seasons due to their shortage.

...rket surveys that were carried out showed that ...dlemen and women who sell snails both inside and ...side the market depend only on the few snails ...nted from the woods during the rainy seasons to ...vice their customers. These opportunities often stop ...ing the dry season (when there is not sufficient rain) ...en there are not enough snails available to be hunted ... maintain market demand.

...il farmers can make up for this shortage by stocking ...ir farms during the rainy season and targeting sales in ... dry seasons when the snails in the woods are often ...rce.

Hotels, restaurants, and various retail outlets for snail meat were noticed to be affected also during the dry seasons. As most of them are out of stock of this delicacy for their customers during these periods. The snail farmer can capitalize by selling directly to this market group. Many snail farmers are making good money by selling parent stock (starting stock) to new farmers. New farmers typically prefer buying their starting stock from established farms that are disease and pest-free as the snails are already adjusted to the farm environment.

There is an international demand for African Giant Land Snails. Snails are being exported to European countries, middle eastern countries (especially Israel), many Asian countries, and the Americas. International contacts and addresses of those who need African snails can easily be obtained from the internet or various offices of chambers of commerce across the country. They can also be gotten on request from commercial offices in various embassies in the country or even from farmers' associations.

International business opportunities have not been capitalized upon by our farmers.

Learning snail farming systems can help farmers take advantage of snail business opportunities inside and outside the country where they reside.

Farmers in local markets must urgently develop scientific methods of rearing snails that can sustain the local demand for snails and also produce a highly improved species of their own types of snails for sale in the International Snail Market.

.

10

CHAPTER

THINGS TO REMEMBER

Number 1: African Giant Land Snail farmers must carefully observe the eggs laid within the farm to make sure the environment is conducive for the eggs to hatch. Eggs typically hatch between 25-45 days. Conditions such as the soil depth and texture may delay hatching. In such cases, artificial scarification should be applied to eggs, to induce hatching.

Number 2: Most African Giant Land Snails reach maturity (the time they can begin to lay eggs) in 4-8 months and typically weigh 90 grams–135 grams.

Number 3: When well cared for, African Giant Land Snails can remain productive over time (they typically live six years or more). This offers farmers an advantage over other livestock with a short lifespan, like poultry. It is also an important factor to note when obtaining financing or when writing a business plan.

Number 4: Good sandy (soft) soil must be used in snail houses before boarding African Giant Land Snails inside the housing. Good sandy soil is essential for the snails to lay eggs and for the eggs to properly hatch. The sand introduced must be up to a height of at least cm to 6 cm high. African Giant Land Snails lay their eggs at a depth of about 2cm to 4 cm deep and hatch with ease when the soil is soft.

Number 5: Remember that African Giant Land Snails hatch on their own. Delay of the egg in hatching might be due to shell thickness or high moisture content of the soil. When the soil within the snail farm is thick and cloggy due to humidity or excessive rain, it becomes difficult for snails to hatch and emerge. Farmers should make sure the right soil content and texture are maintained on the farm.

Number 6: The floor of a snail house should be boarded (case of wood housing) or floored with cement (for block or brick housing) to prevent the snails from burrowing out, thereby causing a significant loss to the farmer.

Number 7: African Giant Land Snails naturally become dormant (aestivate) during hot and dry seasons. Snail farmers can introduce the right environment so that the snails do not sense the change in seasons. This will ensure that they remain productive all year round.

Number 8: African Giant Land Snails have a body mechanism that can self-repair its damaged parts. They can replace damaged organs and other body parts, especially in circumstances where they damage themselves. Regardless, care should be taken to protect snails from damage or harm as it affects their productivity.

Number 9: Weak-looking and sick African Giant Land Snails should be removed immediately from the rest of the stock to avoid a disease epidemic in the farm. Even a single sick snail can cause an outbreak of disease on the farm. Disease outbreaks can cause the farmer time and money to resolve.

Number 10: Farmers should try to source healthy snails when introducing or adding stock to the farm. For example, farmers should avoid purchasing their stock from open markets. Most snails sold in open markets are dehydrated and, in most cases, are in hibernation. They will give the snail farmer very low productivity. The best snails are sourced from a good healthy farm or in the woods when they naturally exist.